PRAISE FOR MOM RULES

"This little treasure for moms will put some inspiring ideas in your mind and a smile on your face!"

—Linda and Richard Eyre, authors of
New York Times #1 bestseller *Teaching Your Children Values*
and founders of ValuesParenting.com

"*Mom Rules* is a delightful instructional manual filled with real-life, sometimes witty, sometimes serious, rules to help moms on their motherhood journey. I recommend it to all moms, no matter what stage in life you find yourself."

—Julie Morgenstern, productivity guru and author of
New York Times bestseller *Organizing from the Inside Out*

"Since kids don't come with instructional manuals, we moms need all the help we can get. That's why *Mom Rules* . . . rules by offering sensible, sanity-saving advice for mothers at any stage of motherhood. A truly great guide for parents everywhere."

—DeAnne Flynn, author of *The Time-Starved Family: Helping
Overloaded Families Focus on What Matters Most*
and *The Mother's Mite: Why Even Our Smallest Efforts Matter*

"*Mom Rules* not only offers great rules and tips on mothering, but is also a reminder that moms (and dads) do 'rule.' Soni and Treion Muller have written a great complement to *Dad Rules* that not only lends perspective and appreciation for the important role of mothers, but also help and encouragement for those in the trenches. In the end, those who will best appreciate this book are the children of the moms that implement these ideas."

—Cheri J. Meiners, author of the
Learning to Get Along children's series

"*Mom Rules* is a timely and positive contribution to parenting, filled with realistic rules, fun stories, and helpful resources. I recommend this delightful manual as the perfect how-to guide to help mothers everywhere manage the ups and downs of parenthood while being better moms."

—Jyl Johnson Pattee, CEO of
Mom It Forward (MomItForward.com)
and cofounder of Evo Conference

MOM
RULES

MOM RULES

SONI & TREION MULLER

PLAIN SIGHT PUBLISHING
An Imprint of Cedar Fort, Inc.
Springville, Utah

ISBN 13: 978-1-4621-1184-8

Published by Plain Sight Publishing, an imprint of Cedar Fort, Inc.,
2373 W. 700 S., Springville, UT 84663
Distributed by Cedar Fort, Inc., www.cedarfort.com

LIBRARY OF CONGRESS CATALOGING-IN-PUBLICATION DATA

Muller, Treion, 1972- author.
Mom rules : because even superheroes need help sometimes / Treion & Soni Muller.
    pages cm
ISBN 978-1-4621-1184-8
1. Child rearing--Handbooks, manuals, etc. 2. Motherhood--Handbooks, manuals, etc. 3. Mother and child. I. Muller, Soni, author. II. Title.
HQ772.M693 2013
306.874'3--dc23

                                        2012048688

Cover design by Erica Dixon
Cover design © 2013 by Lyle Mortimer
Edited and typeset by Michelle Stoll

Printed in the United States of America

10 9 8 7 6 5 4 3 2 1

Printed on acid-free paper

CONTENTS

Thank You

Many of the rules, stories, and anecdotes in this book are thanks to the following moms who have inspired us, whether they know it or not:

Annie Oswald, Penny Stone, Barbara Mordue, Sheridan Larson, Suzette Eaton, Kim Mordue, Karen Mordue, Julianna Morrow, Whitney Permann, Brooke Stone, Glenda Farr, Seletha Shunn Deru, Sandra Anderson, Amy Jolley, Jessica Gibbons, Dana Marchant, Laura Murdoch, Mary Hansen, Misty Stevenson, Amy Andelin, Andrea Johnson, Sarah Anderson, Teresa Farmer, Lindsey Stone, Rebecca Ogden, Jody Hawkins, Terri Fedonczak, Emily Watts, Julie Hanks, Jenny Phillips, and Colleen Loesch.

Thank you for being real women (see Rule 51) and Supermoms.

We also would like to thank Reid Later and Michelle Stoll for their editing brilliance.

BACKGROUND

After the successful release of my (Treion's) instructional manual for dads, *Dad Rules: A Simple Manual for a Complex Job*, I became intrigued by the interest and responses received from some of the moms who bought the book for their husbands. Many would pick it up, page through it, and smile. My curiosity would lead me to ask what they found so amusing. They would always respond in one of two ways (and often in both ways): "My husband could really use this," and, "Many of these rules also apply to me."

Since I am not a mother and do not claim to understand how mothers manage to do so much, I decided then to recruit the best mother I know, my very talented wife, Soni, to coauthor a follow-up book—an instructional manual for moms; a book that could be used in tandem with, and as a complementary partner (pun intended) to, *Dad Rules*, but one that is written with moms in mind and from their perspective. So while my name may be on the cover, I can promise you the words printed on the pages are from the minds and hearts of mothers like you.

INTRODUCTION

Mothers, it's time to accept your true identity. It's time you activate your superpowers and channel the Supermom in you.

While your superpowers probably do not require a mask and cape, nor do they include superhuman strength and the ability to fly, they are just as powerful. Actually, since they are not "make-believe," they are much more powerful.

We know you are probably looking down at your Supermom "costume" right now and saying, "I'm no superhero, just a mother with baby spit-up on my blouse and a house full of chores waiting for me to dive into." We disagree. This is exactly what makes you super. And we want you to recognize and embrace this truth as well.

After all, we have all seen your superpowers in action. Like the superhuman strength it takes to lift a child up onto your hip with one arm while holding a baby carrier with the other and somehow also holding three grocery bags between your two free fingers and the car keys between your teeth. Or the superhuman speed it takes to clean the entire house while doing laundry, putting toddlers down for naps, updating your Facebook status, and still getting dinner done on time. Or the superhuman powers of discernment to realize there is trouble afloat because there is too much silence in the house. Or the superhuman diplomacy it requires to maintain the peace between feuding siblings, all day, every day. On top of all these challenging responsibilities, many of you also successfully manage to work full-time—and sometimes without a sidekick. Phew!

Yes, you are all super, whether you are a married, single, stay-at-home, working, adoptive, or foster mom or grandmother. Regardless of your circumstance, you are the nurturing caregivers to future generations; members of an elite group of sisters going back to mother Eve; a sorority of women worldwide who effectively run your families from brick, wood, mud, and corrugated-steel structures. And women who all answer to the same name—Ma, Moeder, Nene, Mai, Nana, Mutter, Madre, Okaasan, Mamma.

But even superheroes need a helping hand every once in a while—a reminder, a simple manual they can follow. *Mom Rules* is that helping hand—a quick, go-to guide of essential rules to help mothers know what to expect, what to say, and what to do in those difficult moments when they are at their wits' end.

There will be some rules you have already mastered, some that no longer apply, some that may seem extremely obvious, and some you won't like. There may even be rules you choose to ignore or that you disagree with, but when you find yourself in another tricky situation, you'll be grateful you have these rules to come back to.

All eighty-two rules in the book represent years of experiences, study, and mistakes—some from personal experience; some from observing other moms; some from the review of books, blogs, and articles; and some from actually asking other matriarchs how on earth they did it. In other words, this manual is the combined wisdom of many moms who have faced similar challenges and survived.

How you read *Mom Rules* is up to you. Don't think you have to read it cover to cover. It's a manual after all. Go to the sections or rules that interest you. Skip over the rules you feel don't apply (yet) or that you have already mastered. But most of all, as you go over the rules, try to evaluate what type of mom you are and what type of mom you want to be, and then put on your "Supermom" cape and get to work.

Author disclaimer: It is important to note that we have written this book for ourselves as much as we have for you, because we have not mastered many of these rules either. Soni, like many of you, is a "mother-in-motion," who is working on being a better mom each and every crazy day.

> *"I am sure that if the mothers of various nations could meet, there would be no more wars."*
>
> —E. M. Forster, *Howards End*

PART 1

What Moms Should Know

PART 1

What Moms Should Know

Think of this section of the book as a Supermom's orientation to motherhood. Yes, you should know that the Supermom Training Program (STP) begins with the birth of your first child and you only graduate when you die. Oh, and by the way, it is not optional. You are automatically enrolled into the STP as soon as you take that newborn into your arms. You'll also need to know that this program has very few breaks and no pay, just a lot of real-life opportunities to test your superpowers. So why choose to join the program in the first place? Because it's worth it. The greatest force that will elevate you on your journey is love—your love for your children and their love for you. And when you do learn to fly, and you will, you'll come to understand that there is nothing in the world that beats being a mom.

> *"Supermom wasn't a bad job description. The pay was lousy if you were talking about real money. But the payoff was priceless in so many other ways."*
>
> —Roxanne Henke

RULE 1:
Show up for the job every day.

There is no question that being Supermom is the hardest job on the earth. Some men may disagree with this statement, until they have spent a few days alone with the kids and really experience what their wives do and deal with.

If you think about it, not only is a mother a fully participating partner and sometimes acting president of "My Family, Inc.," but she is also the nurse, police officer, and judge (just to name a few roles). But like any successful organization, the family organization can only succeed if the boss is around. Without the consistent and persistent parenting that only a mother can provide, children will suffer and the family may need to turn to arbitration for help.

"Of all sad words of tongue or pen, the saddest are these: 'It might have been!'"

—John Greenleaf Whittier

RULE 2:

Involve your husband in as many of the rules as possible
(aka the Daddy Addendum Rule).

Parenting works best when Mom and Dad are on the same page (or rule). It just does. So whenever you see a rule tagged with the "Daddy Addendum" label, treat it as a gentle reminder for you to involve your husband in that specific rule. This does not mean you should treat him as a child (this is Mom Rules not *Moms* Rule), but rather as an equal partner, who you should think of including in as many parenting responsibilities as possible. Many of the rules in this book also correspond to the same rule numbers in *Dad Rules: A Simple Manual for a Complex Job*, so that Mom and Dad can work on their parenting duties simultaneously if they choose to.

> *"No matter what, Dad was always there with solid words of advice . . . 'Go ask your mother.'"*
>
> —Alan Ray

Rule 3:
Throw up and toxic diapers come with the job.

Unfortunately this is not a misprint. These smelly tasks will be a part of your life forever. At first, newborn baby poop doesn't smell too bad (thanks to a liquid-only diet), and even comes in fun and interesting colors like lime green or mustardy yellow. However, once you introduce real food into your child's diet, things take a dramatic turn for the worst and diaper changing becomes aromatic torture.

And even though teenagers don't typically soil their pants, they are on occasion prone to throwing up, which, as you know, can also be offensive to the senses. To help reduce the amount of toxic cleanup that accompanies the aforementioned task, our family has a dedicated red bucket set aside specifically for this rule. So whenever a child even hints at throwing up, we hand them the red bucket with clear instructions to lie down and only throw up in the bucket or toilet. Easier said than done, we know, but we will continue to try.

Daddy Addendum: Don't forget to involve your husband in this smelly task. Do not let him get away with lame excuses like "I have a sensitive stomach," or "That's not my job." He too must follow this rule and get his hands dirty sometimes. Literally. (See Dad Rule #3.)

Rule 4:
Ask other moms for help.

Mothers have been learning how to be moms from other moms since the beginning, so there's no need for you to attempt to do it alone. Ask for advice, and then find what works for *you*. For starters, turn to the women in your life who have already traversed motherhood. If your own mother, mother-in-law, or grandmother are not available (or a good option), then ask women you admire and respect. There are plenty of amazing moms in every community.

Another great source of help is mommy bloggers. Actually, make that almost four million resources. Yes, that's how many mommy bloggers there are on the Internet today. These moms from around the world contribute their ideas on everything—the right diapers to use, how to decorate your home, how to cook quick and healthy meals, how to raise troubled teens, and everything in between.

Plenty of help is available from other moms who have already learned the hard way and are willing to share their wisdom, so dive in and take advantage of their knowledge. We have included several "Helping hands" references throughout the book that will point you to relevant blogs and websites.

Caution: What you see and read on blogs are typically moms sharing their successes. Remember that they also have challenges, hiccups, and bad days just like you. So when you go online for help, try to also follow Rule 80: "Don't compare yourself to other moms."

> *"My mother phones daily to ask, 'Did you just try to reach me?' When I reply no, she adds, 'So, if you're not too busy, call me while I'm still alive,' . . . and hangs up."*
>
> —Erma Bombeck

RULE 5:
Join a "Moms only" group.

Birds of a feather walk together. There is power in numbers, especially when those numbers are made up of other mothers—women who face similar challenges on their motherhood journey as you. So be a member of an early-morning walking group (like Soni is) or a book club or special-interest groups for scrapbooking, stamps, yoga, or whatever—as long as it provides frequent opportunities to get together with the girls and talk. It can also be an effective stress reliever and therapeutic exercise, if focused on positive and uplifting topics, that is.

Helping Hands: Some great online "moms only" groups that focus their posts, conversations, and even twitter chat sessions on mommy topics are CafeMom .com, MomItForward.com, and PowerOfMoms.com.

RULE 6:
Learn to survive on little sleep.

Whether you are a new mother, one with teen-agers, or even a grandmother, sleep will often be forfeited for crying babies, sick kids, kids in the bed with you, children coming home late from dates, and concern over grandkids. Remember, you gave up the right to a full night's sleep when you became a mother. Call it payback from when you were a kid.

Daddy Addendum: Remember to share this rule with your honey. He too must put in his share of the workload. And if he uses the excuse that he has to go to work the next day, then introduce him to the weekend shift. (See Dad Rule 6.)

> *"[24/7.] Once you sign on to be a mother, that's the only shift they offer."*
>
> —Jody Picoult

Rule 7:

If you hear "I hate you, Mom," it probably means you're doing something right.

You may not like to hear these words from your little sweetheart, but when you do, give yourself a big pat on the back. It probably means you are succeeding as a parent. You have most likely followed through on disciplining your child, and they are not happy about it. What a great opportunity to reinforce the behavior you want them to learn. Respond positively and remind them of why you did or said what you did and that the punishment they are not happy about will continue to be handed out every time they act in a similar fashion. This puts the responsibility and blame back on them, not on their "mean" mother. We like this humorous response one mom gives to her kids when they tell her they hate her: "Nothing you can ever say will change my undying love for you." She gets it.

RULE 8:
Start building a list of "backup" moms.

Sometimes your kids are more likely to listen to advice or constructive criticism from another woman they respect. For instance, a neighbor asked Soni to listen to her son sing and give him candid feedback. The mother felt the son was really pitchy, but he didn't believe his mother. However, the son respected Soni for her singing ability and experience and would more readily listen to her. This rule works especially well with trusted aunties and grandmothers. After you have identified a handful of women in your life whom your kids love and respect, you may want to apprise them of their "backup" status and talk through expectations and potential situations that may arise. Then again, it doesn't have to be that formal at all. A phone call to a "backup" may do the job just as well.

"God could not be everywhere, and therefore he made mothers."

—Jewish proverb

RULE 9:
When everything else fails, turn to the basic needs.

There will be times when your children will have emotional breakdowns, throw tantrums, be extremely grumpy, and literally bounce off the walls. Before you turn to medication, we suggest you first turn to the basics—sleep, food, exercise, and relaxation. Like adults, kids function better if they sleep well, eat healthy, exercise enough, and are not overly stressed. When children are in the middle of playing, they rarely realize they are hungry or tired. They are too lost in their imagination (which is not necessarily a bad thing). However, as you've probably noticed, as soon as they are done playing, they realize how hungry or tired they are. It's usually at these times they behave badly. That's when all they need from you is a healthy supply of the basics.

Helping Hands: Get all the information you need on what is ideal for your child's health and development from KidsHealth.org.

RULE 10:
Don't be afraid to use bribery.

Some parents call it a reward, but when you really break it down, it sometimes looks more like bribery. For example, we have a three-year-old daughter who was very attached to her pacifier (binkie), so much so that we were concerned for the effect it was having on her teeth (as was her dentist). So, knowing how much she loves princess dresses, we took her to a store with a wide variety of lovely princess dresses and asked her to pick out her favorite one. After taking a picture of her and the dress, we promised her she could have it only once she gave up her binkie. Reward or bribery? This works especially well for teenagers. Our nephew was only able to get a cell phone once he completed his Eagle Scout project. Reward or bribery? We'll let you decide.

RULE 11:
If you want it for yourself, hide it.

If you have your eye on a cookie or piece of pie, don't leave it in plain sight. Hide it. If you don't, one of your kids will surely claim it and eat it. Since your children are trickier than you think and will sniff out your regular hiding places, you will need to be sneakier than they are by moving your hiding place regularly. Plus there are locks on doors for a reason. Use them. Treion's mother would lock herself in the bathroom so she could enjoy a candy bar without her two sons begging for some. After finishing her treat she would exit the bathroom with a look of triumph (and a slight smudge of chocolate) on her face.

Dad Rule 11 is "What's yours is theirs." In Mom Rule 11, we cleverly add, "unless they don't know about it."

RULE 12:

Choose between having a supermodel's body and being a mother. You can't have both.

If you think you will be able to have a supermodel physique after you have gone through labor, think again. Besides the overnight appearance of stretch marks and growth of various body parts, you may also lose your hair, break out in acne, and experience irregular body functions. Sounds like fun, doesn't it? Don't despair. While stretch marks never really go away, you can always wear them as a badge of honor for surviving childbirth. Plus the average woman loses around twelve pounds (baby, placenta, fluid) at childbirth and another four to six pounds of water in the first week.[1] So embrace the changes and celebrate motherhood. Because after all, this is what the vast majority of real women in the world look like. And that is more than okay; it is darn-well awesome.

Exception to the rule: There are a small percentage of lucky Supermoms that miraculously manage to be a mom and keep their supermodel body, much to the chagrin of the rest of us moms.

Helping Hands: To learn more about how your body changes after childbirth visit BabyCenter.com and Parents.com.

RULE 13:

Have at least a dozen fun websites or apps on standby.

Sometimes you need to distract your toddlers so you can get something done. Instead of plopping them in front of a movie you could give them something more productive (or at least semi-productive) to do, like playing a game online or on your smartphone where they learn about colors or the alphabet or different country flags.

Helping Hands: Here are some apps and websites you can start with:

Websites: AnimalJam.com, PbsKids.com, NickJr.com, ClubPenguin.com, FunBrain.com.

Apps: Potty Time with Elmo, Bugs and Bubbles, ABC ZooBorns, Let's learn how to draw, Park math, Toddler Flashcards. (There are hundreds to choose from, so choose wisely.)

Rule 14:
Learn to appreciate graffiti…

Because your home will inevitably become a flourishing art exhibit for toddler graffiti. Think about it: Your nice white walls are the prefect canvas for budding artists with lipstick, markers, crayons, and any other traditional or nontraditional writing implements to express themselves. And express themselves they will. So here is a five-step graffiti-appreciation process to help you cope when you discover your toddler's next great masterpiece on your newly painted wall:

Smile. On first discovering waist-high graffiti, shout on the inside and smile on the outside. Remember this is an act of expression and creativity, not defiance or rebellion (unless the child in question is a teenager; then you must apply Rule 56: "Discipline, but do it with love").

Pause. Take a deep breath, count to ten, or twenty, or a hundred. (See Rule 43: "Count to ten, or twenty, or even a hundred before saying something you may regret.")

Teach. Calmly share that certain canvases (paper and coloring books) are acceptable for artistic expression and that others (walls and couches) are not. This may take more than one lesson, but eventually they learn.

Erase. Crayon does come off walls with some soap and water, and even permanent marker can disappear with the help of paint.

Repeat.

Helping Hands: For some ideas on cleaning, check out CleanMama.blogspot.com and AngSays.wordpress.com.

Rule 15:
Be prepared for a potty-training marathon.

Helping your toddler cross the diaper-to-toilet divide will take longer than you think and be more exhausting than you can imagine, but thankfully, it does end. We suggest there are four potty-training phases your munchkin will progress through before they graduate with a porcelain diploma.

Phase 1: Diaper Dumping. Your angel starts pulling off their diaper and dumping it on the floor, or indicating in some other way they are ready to start the big girl or boy poopy process.

Phase 2: Spotty Potty. You spend weeks running your child to the porcelain throne hoping you will make it before they soil their pants. Sometimes you'll make it, and other times you won't. Get ready for many stops and starts.

Phase 3: Pull-Up Pal. Your cowboy or cowgirl will only need a Pull-Up at night while they sleep. This phase can take a long time, because like Phase 2 you have to be prepared to put in the time to move them away from the comfort of the Pull-Up. If you want to get them out of this phase sooner, don't give them a drink before bed. This is harder than it seems because kids are always mysteriously thirsty after you tuck them in. Not an hour before or when you brush their teeth . . . always as you are leaving their room and turning off the light.

Phase 4: Paper Processing. Even once your toddler has stated their potty independence and gets on the throne alone, you still may have to ask them if they are going "peepee" or "poopie." Because if it's the latter you may need to do the paperwork yourself or else you'll end up with spoiled undies, a dirty bum, a clogged toilet, or poop on the bathroom floor. Teaching your child how to wipe properly is also an essential step during this phase. (We just had this discussion again with our seven-year-old who uses far too much paper, which tends to clog up the toilet and cause it to overflow. Yucky.)

Rule 16:

For safety and sanity reasons,
hide all scissors and sharp objects.

On one memorable occasion after Soni had fallen asleep on the couch, our three-year-old decided it would be nice to give Mommy a hair cut. So after retrieving a pair of scissors from the kitchen drawer, she proceeded to cut Soni's bangs. Luckily she wasn't too far into the "extreme makeover" before Soni woke up. On another occasion, our young nephew cut a neighbor's expensive blouse that she had just bought in Paris (France, not Idaho), before proudly proclaiming, "I just cut your shirt, lady." Besides the shredding of important documents, curtains, money, shoelaces, and your favorite blouse, scissors (or any sharp object) are simply not safe for children to play with, so make sure you hide them where little hands cannot find them.

RULE 17:

Remember, it's your daughter's wedding—NOT yours

This may be hard to hear, but remember that this is your daughter's wedding, not your "how I would have done it if I could do it all over again" redemption song. And that's all we dare say about that.

RULE 18:

Keep your husband out of the wedding plans altogether.

Trust us, it's for your own good. But do this without hurting his feelings. Sure, your husband can be involved . . . in paying the bills, being assigned as the official Wedding Gopher (an official title used by wedding planners worldwide that is specifically assigned to fathers), and showing up for the wedding. When it comes to weddings, the only thing worse than breaking Rule 17 is forgetting to follow this one. Don't believe us? Watch *Father of the Bride*.

Exception to the rule: Some dads are cool, calm, and collected enough to be involved. Treion is not one of these dads, but we know they are out there . . . somewhere.

RULE 19:
Be okay with your sons wearing pink.

In *Dad Rules*, the corresponding rule is "Be okay with wearing pink." For many years, pink was primarily connected to the female gender. This has changed over the past few years. Pink is a powerful color today and is associated with worthy causes like breast-cancer awareness. It has become such an acceptable color that even tough National Football League (NFL) players accessorize their uniforms with pink gloves, laces, socks, and bicep bands during October in honor of Breast Cancer Awareness Month. In our extended family, we proudly wear pink in memory of our darling little niece Lily. Her older brothers even wear pink slippers, pink T-shirts, pink bracelets, and her pink princess backpack to junior high and high school. In other words, don't be afraid of buying your son a pink polo shirt or shorts or tie, because there is no longer a gender color divide.

RULE 20:
Learn to love carpooling.

You're going to be spending a lot of time in the car driving your kids and their friends around. You might as well learn to like it. Some moms play games like "I spy" or "slug bug." Some play sing-along songs, and some pepper the passengers with questions. One friend played language-learning CDs, and the kids in her carpool actually learned basic Russian while driving to and from activities. Find your groove, whatever it is, and enjoy the ride.

Helping Hands: For ideas on what games you can play in the car, check out MomsMinivan.com.

Daddy Addendum: Share some of the carpool duties with Dad so he can also share in the joy. (See Dad Rule 20.)

Rule 21:
There's never a satisfactory answer to "why."

So don't expect your young child to stop asking you "why?" It's simply the question that doesn't have an answer and never, ever ends. Until one day it does, usually when your son or daughter is old enough to realize they have all the answers—and then you have a whole other set of challenges (covered in Rule 23). It's about this time that you miss being trapped in the never-ending "why?" game because at least then you were seen as someone who knew all the answers.

Rule: 22:
Start a savings account for each child.

Children are expensive, and they cost more the older they get. It starts with diapers and formula and progresses to everyday clothing and then to annual gymnastics and sports uniforms. Then come the high-ticket items like orthodontics, prom dresses, and car insurance. Teach your children to help save for their future by putting half of everything they receive into their own savings account. Over time, these small deposits add up. Some moms use piggy banks, some open up real bank accounts, and some create their own banks. One family we know teaches their kids all about finance management and responsibility with the "Two Fish Bank." They use a simple spreadsheet where their kids can see how much money they have earned and how much they can spend.

Helping Hands: For a great family-friendly tool that teaches your kids about finance management, check out Famzoo.com.

Mommy Data: In 2010 the average total family expense of a child through age 17 was $323,380. In the United States, the average cost to attend college in 2010–2011 was between $7,605 and $27,293 (per year), not including room and board.[2] That's potentially over $100,000 for a four-year degree!

RULE 23:
All kids think they are geniuses.

Accept it. There is a phase, sometimes a decades-long phase, when your children will have all the answers, know everything, and do everything by themselves. We tease our nephew for the way he expresses his displeasure toward his mom whenever she tries to tell him something. His automatic response is usually, "Gosh! Mom!" which is accompanied by a habit covered in Rule 27: eye rolling. There is no fix for this. We just thought you ought to know you are not alone, your kids are normal, and there is nothing you can do about it.

RULE 24:
No matter how bad it looks, hair will grow back.

Chances are one of your children will choose to trim, buzz, or color their own hair, which usually does not turn out the way they had planned. In that moment of shock when you first see the failed makeover, remember these four words: hair will grow back. There is, unfortunately, also a chance that your young child will cut Mommy's hair while she is taking a nap (see Rule 16). Remembering this rule will reduce the trauma when you wake up and realize that not even your hairdresser can put the disaster back together again.

Mommy Tip: Learn to cut hair. Hairdresser (or barber) is one of the many job titles moms should proudly claim. You never know when you'll need to fix a failed attempt.

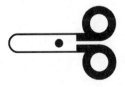

RULE 25:
Become a competent chef.

When we got married, Soni could only make a handful of meals, most from a box or can. Now, thanks to recipe books and Food Network, she is an accomplished chef who can quickly whip up a number of healthy meals and treats. She owns more recipe books than the Library of Congress and frequently surprises the family with new (and usually wonderful) meals.

But some of our family favorites are the ones we invent ourselves, like "Barney Blood" smoothies, named by the kids because of the purple color of the drink. (Ingredients: Spinach, mixed frozen berries, and apple or orange juice.)

Helping Hands: There are so many great mommy blogs and websites you can turn to for help with this rule. Some of our favorites are OurBestBites.com, MomsWhoThink.com, and SimplyLivingSmart.com. But just Google "mommy food blogs" and you'll be introduced to a world of possibilities.

> *"The most remarkable thing about my mother is that for thirty years she served the family nothing but leftovers. The original meal has never been found."*
>
> —Calvin Trillin

RULE 26:

Your kids are never too old for bedtime stories or chats.

One of the saddest days in raising a child is the day they no longer want to be read a story before bedtime. It usually means they feel they are too old. But don't give up. That cherished time you have with your child just before bed does not need to disappear. Instead of bedtime stories, you can take a few minutes every night just talking to each kid and staying in touch. Thanks to this rule, we recently learned how much our nine-year-old loves learning about geology. We had no idea our little gymnast had such a passion for mountains and unusual rock formations.

This rule also works especially well with teenagers coming home from late-night dates and activities with friends. Many moms shared how important it was to check in with their kids at times like these. It kept them in the loop and helped their children be accountable because they knew Mom (or Dad) was going to be waiting up for them and making sure they were all right.

RULE 27:
Don't take
eye-rolling personally.

This behavior happens so often in the adolescent years that you cannot afford to take it personally. Just think of it as a natural side effect found in most youth that usually fizzles out in the early twenties . . . usually. If you really want to freak your kids out, start doing it yourself. Besides really bugging them, this has been known to put an end to the practice, probably because they don't want to see mom doing it anymore.

Rule 28:
Stress less about the mess.

If there is one thing all parents should know about children, it's that they are messy. They spill soda on the carpet, wipe their sticky hands on the couch, shove food under their beds, drop dirty clothes all over their rooms, leave shoes in the yard, and throw candy wrappers on the floor.

This is one of the most common themes we have heard from the moms we've spoken to. Our question to you is, if this is common knowledge, why do we still stress so much about it? Maybe we think that our kids will be different. Maybe we believe constant nagging, discipline, or bribery (see Rule 10) will exorcize them of these bad habits. Maybe not. Do what you can, but remember that stressing about the mess and the delinquents that caused it won't help; it'll just give you heartburn and gas.

RULE 29:
Give the "chef" a break sometimes.

Okay, sometimes moms just need to get out of the house—away from the messy kitchen and tiresome chores. There will be times when the thought of making another meal for a tiny audience that doesn't appreciate your efforts will drive you completely batty. If the only solution involves dropping by the local fast-food restaurant, then go ahead and break Rule 25. But for heaven's sake, choose the apple slices over fries and the milk over soda. Yes, if you must go out for fast food, go with the healthier choices.

Daddy Addendum: This may be a good time to activate Dad Rule 25. If your husband can't crack an egg or mix up some mac & cheese, then teach him how to cook up at least six "go to" meals he can use at times like this.

RULE 30:
Stay one step ahead of the game.

Life with kids can seem like a crazy ten-ring circus with some kids doing homework, some going to soccer practice, some taking piano lessons, some needing to be fed, some needing sleep, and others trashing the house. If you are not a vigilant ring-master in keeping the circus running properly, then things can get out of hand. One way to stay ahead of the circus is to plan together as a family—set time aside to go over the week's schedule, including chore assignments, lessons, games, homework, play time, and family activities. It is during that time you try to anticipate where things can go wrong and what to do at those times. While we are not the poster family for this rule, there are several moms we know who could vie for that award. How they do it? That, sisters, is a whole other book, but remember to turn to Rule 4 and the many wonderful helping hands in your community and online.

Helping Hands: Julie Morgenstern is a mom that not only follows this rule, but also owns it. She has even been called the "queen of putting people's lives in order" by USA Today. Learn more about how she does it at JulieMorgenstern.com.

PART 2

What Moms Should Say

PART 2

What Moms Should Say

I n this section, you'll learn when to activate your Supermom ears and when to deactivate your mouth, as well as a handful of other rules to remind you of what to say and when to say it.

Whether you like it or not, your children are your apprentices, your Superkids in training. They watch you to learn how to behave and what they should say and do in certain situations. No pressure. Actually, being a mom is one of the most influential roles in the world. Supermom comes with high expectations, and in the eyes of your children, that's who you are, even if they don't tell you as much.

RULE 31:
Learn when to say nothing at all.

This may be a difficult rule to follow, because we all have the answer or piece of advice for most situations. After all, we've successfully survived childhood, including our teenage years, and we know what's best for our children. Right? Well, yes and no! Yes, because that statement is technically correct. No, because when emotions are involved, your children don't care what you experienced thirty years ago.

Recently we were introduced to the emotional (and irrational) side of our oldest daughter—you know, where nothing you say seems to help. There's a whole lot of crying and babbling and crazy talk. It requires a lot of effort to give her room to talk through her perceived issue without interfering. Plus, attempting to offer advice or reasoning during times like these simply does not help.

So to kick off this section on what moms should say, we suggest sometimes saying nothing at all. Because many times there really isn't anything you could say that would help anyway. However, practicing good listening skills will always benefit you, the volatility of the situation, and especially the child you are honoring by following this rule (which can be applied to many non-parental situations in life as well).

Daddy Addendum: If you think this rule is hard for you, imagine how difficult it is for Dad. Men typically like to fix things (and people) with logic, a clear set of instructions, and macho determination. Unfortunately, this approach doesn't work well with children (or people in general). So remind your dear husband of this important rule often. For more help for dads on this rule, see Dad Rule 31.

RULE 32:

If you don't know, then say, "I don't know."

If you don't know how far the moon is from Earth or what the fundamental theorem of calculus is, say so. If you cannot remember these and a gazillion other interesting facts, figures, and general-knowledge questions your children may ask you, say so. Kids are smart enough, especially in their teenage years, to know this is the case. So be honest with them. Admitting you are not the all-knowing Mother Goose will get you major points with your children (unless you're just saying it to brush them off). Nothing is more annoying than a know-it-all, especially if that person happens to be your mom (or dad). However, make sure you follow up your genuine admission of knowledge deficit with the offer to help them discover the answer. Fortunately, many of us have smartphones on hand or home computers to help us find the answer to some questions very quickly. Or even better, encourage your kids to search for the answers themselves. It's a great opportunity for you to learn something new together.

Helping Hands: Resources like Wikipedia and the Merriam-Webster Dictionary are a must for every mom.

Rule 33:
When you mess up, say, "I'm sorry."

This is another rule that will endear your children to you. You are not perfect. You make mistakes like everybody else. You know it, and they know it, so why not teach your children a valuable lesson by sincerely saying you're sorry when you mess up? One mom shared how she would apply this rule on the mornings she would argue with her kids. After her kids left for school, she would have time to reflect on how she could have dealt with a particular situation better and then write that child a note and drop it off at the school office. The kids would then be called to the office to get the note with their mom's apology. When they got home, Mom would be there with arms open wide and a fresh start.

"Apology is a lovely perfume; it can transform the clumsiest moment into a gracious gift."

—Margaret Lee Runbeck

RULE 34:
When your child is right, say so.

Regardless of how difficult it may be to take advice and correction from your children, sometimes it is the right thing to do. However, in order for this rule to work properly, you first have to give them permission to help you be a better mom. Ask them to tell you when you are not treating them like you should or when you stand in need of correction. Second, have the courage to listen to their comments and suggestions without being defensive. Children can be brutally honest, but sometimes that is exactly what we need to hear. Last, change your behavior.

Rule 35:
Never say, "Because I said so, that's why."

This statement can be an automatic response for many of us if preceded by persistent nagging on the part of our kids. We may start off the dialogue by calmly and patiently responding to our child's request, but after a continuous string of whining, the words "because I said so, that's why" seem to involuntarily flow from our lips, as if to say, "And that is final." Since this statement usually ends the discussion, we naturally think it works, so we return to it more often and earlier on in future discussion.

But think about how much this same statement bugged you when you were a kid. It disrespects the intelligence of your child and communicates that you don't want them to think for themselves. If you really don't want to debate or discuss something with your children, tell them that instead. That way, you at least show them respect and you're not being rude.

Daddy Addendum: Encourage Dad to also follow this rule to avoid being too annoying. (See Dad Rule 35.)

RULE 36:

Live with gratitude in your heart and on your tongue.

There is so much to be grateful for—good health, food, clothes, shelter, safety, and an abundant life. Children who hear their parents express gratitude and appreciation often tend to follow suit and feel less entitled to material possessions. We were both delighted and surprised to hear our two-year-old start saying "please," "thank you," and "you're welcome" all in the same sentence—delighted because he must be learning it somewhere; surprised because, while we try to follow this rule, we are not sure we are the people he has learned it from. So who has he been learning it from? To practice this rule ourselves, we would like to thank our extended family and friends for setting the example for little TJ. To quote a well-known African proverb, "It (really does) take a village to raise a child."

RULE 37:
Don't talk negatively about your body.

Especially around your daughters, because you don't want them to become self-conscious about their own perceived imperfections and turn to extremes like eating disorders. Especially around your sons, because you want them to respect and revere women for the characteristics and qualities that matter, like personality and kindness, not the ones that don't, like physique. Soni has made it a point that we never use the word "fat." Even with terms like "I feel fat," or "I have gained weight," or "That will make me fat." While people typically use these terms in reference to themselves, it usually comes across negative and self-degrading. Love who you are and the body you have been endowed with, and express that positive self-image through your words.

RULE 38:
Say "I love you" often.

There is no question that carrying a child through pregnancy and then going through the indescribable pain of childbirth is a clear sign you love your children. There are also many other acts you moms perform each day that show love for your children, like feeding them, changing diapers, and picking up after them. Not to mention being willing to sacrifice your life if it could save theirs. Yes, you know you love them, but they still need to hear it, often. Though actions do speak louder than words, sometimes children haven't learned the right language yet for them to understand what your actions mean. Sincerely looking a child in the eyes and telling them you love them gives them an immediate lift and reinforces all of the things you do for them on a daily basis.

"If I were asked to define Motherhood, I would have defined it as Love in its purest form. Unconditional Love."

—Revathi Sankaran

RULE 39:
Let your children hear you tell your husband that you love him.

Like the previous rule, your children need to hear you tell your husband that you love him. Do it especially if it makes them uncomfortable. We do a good job of making our kids uncomfortable by hugging, kissing, and dancing around in the kitchen while saying, "I love you." We also go our separate ways each morning with a kiss and those three words. This is one rule we can confidently say we are following. Wish we could say that about more of the rules.

RULE 40:
Try to say "yes" as much as possible.

Yes. There really is no sweeter-sounding word to a child because it opens up windows of opportunity and fun for them. The refreshing utterance of "yes" communicates you trust them and want them to be happy. So often they ask and we say "no" even before the question has left their lips. Instead of automatically pulling out the "no" card, why not look for ways you can say "yes"?

Our oldest had been babysitting for us and asked if she could play night games with some of her friends until late. It was on a Saturday night and we usually prefer her going to bed early since we have church the next morning. But we said "yes" because she had been such a great help to us and deserved the reward. While what we did was really no big deal, she appreciated hearing *yes* so much that it really went a long way. *Yes* can also precede a conditional statement— like "after you have finished your piano practice," or "if you first help your brother with his homework"— but so can the word *can't*. See the next rule for why *yes* is always the better option.

RULE 41:
Try to eliminate "can't" from your vocabulary.

This rule works best when used with the previous rule. But it can be one of the most difficult rules to follow, because there are so many things your kids shouldn't do that it's easy to blurt out the words, "No, you can't." Instead, empower your child by saying, "We've discussed this before, what do you think?" Or, "Sure you can, after you have finished your chores and homework."

This response is a positive affirmation instead of a negative directive that still gets them to complete their agreed-upon chores. Plus, "can't," "cannot," and "No," can have the complete opposite effect with teenagers. They hear "can't" and think, "I'll show you." But when they are asked to think for themselves, they have a much better chance of choosing the right.

> *"The best way to keep children at home is to make the home atmosphere pleasant, and let the air out of the tires."*
>
> —Dorothy Parker

Rule 42:
Learn when to say the right thing at the right time.

Unlike Rule 31, there are many times when you should say something, but *when* to say that something is the tricky part. A friend of ours confessed that this rule was one she really struggles with. "I always say things at the wrong times," she admitted. "My kids get so mad and tell me, 'Thanks, Mom. Why did you have to tell me that right now? I am going to feel like crap the whole day.'" In many cases saying what needs to be said can be done later or at a better time. This will be tough to figure out, so "when in doubt, wait it out."

RULE 43:

Count to ten, or twenty, or even a hundred before saying something you may regret.

Follow this rule when attempting to follow the previous rule. It may save you a whole bunch of regrets. There is also nothing wrong with saying, "We're going to talk about this later," and then walking away from the situation while you count to a hundred to calm down. This gives you time to think about what you are going to say, so you do not speak out of anger or frustration.

"A soft answer turneth away wrath."

—Proverbs 15:1

RULE 44:

The answer to, "Mom, can I show you something?" is always, "Yes!"

If you take the time to watch your children skip, do endless jumps, ride their bikes with no hands, and other kid stuff when they are young, they will more likely allow you to be involved in their lives when they are older. We think that's a fair trade, don't you?

> *"In a child's eyes, a mother is a goddess. She can be glorious or terrible, benevolent or filled with wrath, but she commands love either way. I am convinced that this is the greatest power in the universe."*
>
> —N. K. Jemisin

RULE 45:
Start all lectures by bringing up a positive behavior first.

One mom shared how she began applying this rule after she had given her son a lecture and he had responded by saying, "What else am I doing wrong?" His sincere question helped her realize that to him it appeared as if she was only focusing on his negative behaviors instead of also looking for the many good things he was doing as well. This motivated her to change her approach to parenting and reduced the amount of "lectures" she gave. By actively seeking and recognizing positive behavior in her children, she noticed that their behavior also improved, which required less correcting on her part anyway.

Daddy Addendum: Invite your hubby to read Rule 45 on this topic as well, "If you feel the urge to lecture, stop and think about it first."

RULE 46:
Get used to saying,
"Go look again."

Your kids will not be able to find anything you ask them to look for. They will walk into a room, look around, and come out saying they couldn't find it. One strategy that seems to work in regard to this very common condition of selective blindness is to tell them to go look again or you'll charge them a quarter if you find it yourself. We promise that after a while, they'll start to look harder.

RULE 47:
Never gossip.

Gossiping is a deceptive companion. It can feel so good and warm and comfy because you are turning attention away from your own imperfections and issues. But it is also an unattractive trait that can turn you, and your children who see your example, into bitter people. Especially important: never, ever gossip with your children about another child in the family. It destroys trust and the sanctity of the family unit.

"One of the most important ways to manifest integrity is to be loyal to those who are not present. When you defend those who are absent, you retain the trust of those present."

—Stephen R. Covey

RULE 48:
Remember to laugh.

At life, at your children, and at yourself. Because if you don't find humor in the messiness and madness of motherhood, you will probably cry a lot instead. As mothers know, there is sometimes a very thin line between laughing and crying. Choose the happy side of that line.

RULE **49**:

Don't say anything you wouldn't
want your grandmother to hear.

Whenever you are in doubt about what to say,
remember this rule. It should be easy enough
if you just imagine your grandmother is a witness to
the conversation. If you wouldn't say it in her pres-
ence, don't say it.

Rule 50:

If what you are saying isn't getting across, try saying it differently.

Your children, especially teenagers, have a tendency to ignore the positive comments you make and focus instead on the critical. If you are trying to get your point across and your teen isn't getting it, it's your responsibility to change the delivery method. Don't just keep saying the same thing over and over.

A mom was talking to her thirteen-year-old about how she needed to improve her math grades. What her daughter heard was "You are not getting enough A's." What the mom thought she was saying was, "You are an A student, and if you are not getting As, we need to figure out why." After realizing they were not connecting, the mom stopped and realized she had to say it differently. In doing so, she took the fight out of her daughter so they could start the discussion over again, but this time from the same side. Sometimes just acknowledging that the words are getting in the way of the intent will alleviate many situations.

PART 3

What Moms
Should Do

PART 3

What Moms Should Do

In this last section, we dig a little deeper into what Supermoms can do to ensure their children are happy and successful. In the previous section, we covered almost twenty rules related to what moms should say. But that is all in vain if you don't follow through on what you said you would do. Children are very forgiving, up to a point. If you let them down too often, you may lose their trust in you. So make sure you align what you say with what you do.

> *"Happiness is when what you think, what you say, and what you do are in harmony. Always aim at complete harmony of thought and word and deed. Always aim at purifying your thoughts and everything will be well."*

> —Gandhi

Rule 51:
Be a real woman.

While we sometimes like to be entertained by the eccentric, bizarre, and unusual, we have to give credit to the real women of the world—women who put family first, are true to their marriage vows, and are considerate and kind. Women who are as steady as a rock, but also as delicate as a flower. Women who don't seek after what the entertainment industry calls happiness, but who instead look for the lasting joys in this life that come from family time. These are the qualities of real superheroes, but because they are not flashy or sensational, they rarely make it into the movies.

Helping Hands: Buy the Supermom action figure (yes there is one) for yourself or for other Supermoms: HappyWorker.com/Supermom.

RULE 52:

Don't blame your child's teacher
for your child's bad grades.

Except with rare exceptions, this responsibility lies with you. While it may be a teacher's responsibility to teach the fundamentals, it is your duty (along with Dad) to take the time to ensure that those fundamentals are understood and practiced. It is called homework for a reason. With the national US student-to-teacher ratio being somewhere between 15:1 and 17:1,[3] teachers just don't have the capacity to give each student enough attention to ensure success. That responsibility has always been with parents anyway. So if your child is struggling, you need to be the one to step in and help. If you don't have the knowledge to help, find a tutor; if you cannot afford a tutor, try turning to online tools and solutions for help.

Helping Hands: One great online tutoring site is KhanAcademy.org, and it's free.

RULE 53:

If the technology doesn't include your kids, put it away.

There is a time and place for checking your Facebook time line or favorite blog site. There is also a time to put the smartphone or tablet away, turn off the computer, and spend time with your children. Decide beforehand what time you'll spend online and what time you'll spend with family, and then honor that schedule. One mom who spends a lot of time for work on her computer was tired of brushing off her kids so she could work. She decided she would get up an hour earlier each morning to work, which wasn't easy. Then as soon as she heard her kids get up in the morning, she would immediately turn off the computer and focus on them. After some time of doing this, she noticed that her kids were behaving better because they weren't competing with the computer for her attention.

RULE 54:
Believe in magic.

Because it is alive and well in your children. It's the kind of magic that empowers them to paint anything, build anything, sing anything, imagine anything, be anyone, and do anything. When our little Ruby started preschool, she was instructed to use crayons to draw herself. When she was done she was all purple and pink, her favorite princess colors. The teachers politely told her that people are not really that color and that she should use different colors. We disagreed. If she saw herself as a purple and pink princess, then that's exactly how we wanted her to look on paper. Unfortunately, this magic slowly fizzles out and eventually dies as kids get older. Do whatever you can to encourage your children to hold onto that magic and continue to color outside the lines. Sometimes kids just need to be given a pencil, paper, and some tape and be encouraged to use their imagination, because this is how magic happens.

> *"Listen to the Mustn'ts, child, listen to the Don'ts.*
> *Listen to the Shouldn'ts, the Impossibles, the Won'ts.*
> *Listen to the Never Haves, then listen close to me.*
> *Anything can happen, child. Anything can be."*
>
> —Shel Silverstein

RULE 55:
Raise children, not clones of you.

You may have a PhD from the "school of hard knocks" and want your children to pick up where you left off, but don't deprive them of difficult life lessons that will mold and shape them into who they can become. Encourage them to find their own passion, and don't force your paradigms and opinions on them. We saw this rule in practice with a friend's family of four boys. After having three athletic, sports-loving boys, the fourth son surprised them by not being interested in sports at all. Instead he walked around singing movie tunes and building elaborate contraptions with duck tape and cardboard. Instead of forcing him to play on a soccer or basketball team, they quickly recognized his unique interests and talents and encouraged him in those areas.

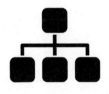

Rule 56:
Discipline,
but do it with love.

Kids will be kids. They will spill a gallon of paint in your minivan even after you warned them not to play with it (true story). They will hit their younger sibling, sneeze all over the birthday cake, lose just one of their new shoes, start a fire in the backyard, and engage in an endless number of other very annoying behaviors.

While not all childhood behaviors require disciplining, some do. Kids need you to be clear on what is appropriate and what is not. While there are many wonderful books that go into depth on how parents should discipline their children, the one rule we suggest you always follow is to do it with love. No matter what a child has done, there is always room for love. Even in the midst of severe punishment, parents can still love the child while also holding them accountable for the behavior.

Helping Hands: Receive weekly emails and tips on this rule from the authors of "Parenting With Love and Logic" at LoveAndLogic.com.

RULE 57:
Power tools
also come in pink.

Yes, drills, circular saws, and nail guns may typically be Daddy toys, but sadly, in a world where nearly half of all marriages end in divorce, possessing basic skills with power tools is not only liberating but may also be a necessary skill. And even if you are married, putting together the bookshelf yourself is a great way to show your husband who's really the boss and show your kids that moms are tougher than they think.

Helping Hands: Learn from these DIY moms—FixItMoms.com and TheDiyMommy.com.

RULE 58:
Teach your kids the art of being thrifty.

Even if you can afford not to be thrifty, teach your kids this valuable lesson. You never know where life may lead them, and it's never a bad idea to reuse, repurpose, repaint, refinish, and revamp. Go to garage sales and thrift stores with your children and find pieces of furniture, clothing, and other stuff you can work on together. Sometimes the best "deals" are the ones you make, fix up, and decorate yourself.

Helping Hands: A great mommy blog that represents this rule is AllThingsThrifty.com. Learn from momma Brooke and her family how they do it.

RULE 59:

When you go out, take one of your children with you.

Unless you have been with them all day and you need a break; then send Dad with them. However, if you are able and emotionally willing, having one of your offspring tag along is always a good idea. It affords you the one-on-one time and attention that is always so important in a child's life. But make sure you use that time to talk to your child and not listen to the radio or talk to other people on your phone.

We know the parents of a Down-syndrome kid who are wonderful examples of this rule. Even though they are both retired and their son is in his thirties, they take him with them. It's really inspirational to see him loaded into the truck on the way to go camping, shopping, fishing, or to garage sales with Mom and Dad.

Daddy Addendum: Involve Dad in this rule as well. Sometimes sending one of the kids with him provides you with just enough of a break to be able to make it through the day. (See Dad Rule 59.)

RULES 60:
Capture the memories.

With all the amazing advances in technology, including free blogging and journaling tools, and the fact that most of us have a camera on our phones, there really is no excuse for not following this rule. Even if you are not into scrapbooking, and Soni is not, there are several digital alternatives that allow you to print a hardbound book from your Facebook time line, Twitter feed, photo library, or blog.

This may be one of the most important and fun rules for moms to follow. Just think of all the funny things your children say and do. If you are quick, you may be able to capture those things on your camera phone; if not, you can always write about it on your blog or Facebook time line. One of these memories captured by a mom was between her young daughter and a friend. While trying to remove a lid from a jam jar, one said to the other, "I can't get the yid off," to which the other replied, "It's not a yid, it's a wid."

We know you have dozens of these small but memorable moments too. Don't lose them, capture them! Whether it's with the camera or the pen doesn't matter, as long as you have some record you can use to embarrass them on their wedding day.

Helping Hands: Some websites to help you capture the memories include MyJotJournal.com, TweetBookz .com, Shutterfly.com, Everything2print.sharedbook.com, Snapfish.com, and Blurb.com.

Rule 61:
Be social-media smart.

There is a lot you can learn about your kids by what they post on social-media sites. Think about it. They are generally much more open with their friends than with you, so being connected with your kids will allow you to be the proverbial "fly on the wall." It will also alert you to potentially embarrassing moments and behavioral issues. Warning: Be connected but not addicted.

Mommy Data: According to teens, parents who use social media are more likely to talk with their teen about what kinds of things should and should not be shared online or on a cell phone. Teens report that parents who are friends with their teens on social media are more likely to have these conversations than parents who have not friended their child (92 percent versus 79 percent).[4]

RULE 62:
Protect your kids from harmful online influences.

We've already shared the good about technology—social media, blogging, and digital scrapbooking. But there is also a dark side to the Web that is ever expanding. Pornography, violent gaming, sexting, and online stalkers are but a few of these bad elements. Do everything you can to protect and teach your children about them. If you follow Rule 1, you'll also be able to see the warning signs more readily. A mother who was vigilantly following this rule was able to warn her daughter about a potentially dangerous encounter online. After severing the relationship immediately, the daughter told her Mom, "Thanks, Mom, for bringing me to my senses." Remember, your life experiences equip you to spot potentially dangerous situations your children may not be able to recognize. It's your job to bring them to their senses.

Helping Hands: Some websites that provide wonderful data, tips, and resources on how to protect your kids include SafeKids.com, UKnowKids.com, and YourSphereForParents.com.

RULE 63:
Raise service-centered kids.

We recently heard about a man named Stephen who sacrificed almost everything, including a promising career, to dedicate himself to an orphanage in his home country of Kenya. As we listened to his inspirational story and how it truly blessed the lives of these little children, one of our daughters looked at us and with such sincerity, said, "I want to do something to help those children. Maybe I'll go around the neighborhood collecting shoes and clothes." This was one of those rewarding moments you cherish as a parent. We have tried to teach our children to look outward—to look for others who are in need and then do their best to fill that need. It's amazing how much children grow when they are focused on helping others.

Helping Hands: Google the term "children philanthropists" and witness the inspirational results of what happens when mothers follow this rule.

RULE 64:
Be there at the crossroads, or your kids may get lost.

Remember Rule 1? If you are showing up for the job everyday, you will also be following this rule. It is so important to your children that you be there for their first soccer game, date, driving lesson, kiss (at least around to tell you about it), and everything else in between. Be the stabilizing force, the steady rock, in a world of constant change. If you are not there for them at the crossroads, they may make a wrong turn and get lost. Plus, you may miss out on moments like this: On putting her daughter to bed, this mom told her daughter that it was bedtime and she needed to be quiet. To this, her four-year-old fired right back with, "Yeah, you gotta be quiet except for burps, farts, and scratches. And we don't get out of bed except for throw-ups and bleeds." Classic.

RULE 65:
Be a messenger of hope.

A mother is hope personified. Her role begins as a creator, and she spends the remainder of her days nurturing, loving, comforting—whispering words of encouragement and hope throughout her child's life. Be that messenger who speaks of what can be, for your children will need someone to look up to if everything and everyone else fails them. Treion's mother was one such lady. Even though they lived in trailer parks and there was not a lot of hope for a better life, she always encouraged Treion to fulfill his potential and dream big. It was this messenger of hope that raised him to where he is today.

"Hope is the thing with feathers—
That perches in the soul—
And sings the tune without the words—
And never stop—at all—"

—Emily Dickinson

Rule 66:

If you have room to love another child, consider adopting.

There are so many children (young and old) who need the love and stability that only a family can provide. After having three daughters of their own, some friends of ours chose to adopt a girl and her twin brothers, literally doubling their family overnight. Over the past few years we have watched as this family has loved and embraced these new additions, welcoming them to their family. Treion's "surrogate" mom said it best, "Bearing children is very different than 'birthing' children. I have not only been blessed with birthing five children of my own, but I have also had the privilege of being the mom to a couple of other children. With them I have also been able to bear their sorrows, feel their joys, and rejoice in their successes." Thanks, Mom, for being there for me.

Helping Hands: If this rule appeals to you, then you may like the list of the top adoption blogs by parents found on CircleOfMoms.com.[5]

Rule 67:
Have frequent one-on-one talks with each child.

The more children you have and the older they get, the harder it is to follow this rule. With five children, we have to be creative in how we spend time with the kids. Sometimes it's while doing dishes together, going grocery shopping, working in the garden, and just before bedtime. One great example of living this rule is from a mom who has a set lunch date with her teenage son every week, where she picks him up from school and takes him to his favorite restaurant. That way, no matter how much homework or extracurricular activities he has, she knows she has his undivided attention at least once a week. Go Supermom!

Daddy Addendum: Dad also needs to follow this rule in order to have a healthy relationship with his children. (See Dad Rule 67.)

Rule 68:

Remember that your relationship
with your child is more important
than punctuality, possessions,
or other people.

Your kids will make bad decisions (see Rule 77)
and embarrass you in public. They will throw
tantrums in the grocery aisle, call strangers "stupid,"
and post pictures on Facebook that will make you
blush. You can lose it and scream at your teenage
daughter to show the world you are in charge, or you
could take time to pause and remember who you are
and who you are responsible for raising. Screaming at
your daughter to get in the car so that you are not late
for a soccer game is not worth the damage it could do
to your relationship with her, even if you are ten minutes late. She is much more important than being on
time for a dumb game. Remember, people are more
important than things, relationships are more important than time, and your children are more important
than what people think about you.

*"Never let a problem to be solved become more im-
portant than a person to be loved."*

—Thomas S. Monson

RULE 69:
Celebrate your children.

Each child has unique skills, talents, and gifts. Some may sing like a bird, do back handsprings like an Olympic gymnast, crack impossible mathematical equations like Einstein, or paint like Picasso. And some may have skills or talents not as outwardly apparent. Maybe they can light up a room with their charisma, have the compassion of Mother Teresa, or possess the ability to make anyone feel comfortable. Regardless of who they are, it is our responsibility to celebrate their uniqueness. Look for opportunities to spotlight your children's gifts and talents by celebrating those attributes often. One mom shared how she saw this rule exemplified in Israel. She witnessed how a whole extended family came together to celebrate a Jewish boy's coming of age celebration (Bar Mitzvah). She watched as he was hoisted onto his uncle's shoulders and carried with pride along the street. Seeing the joy on his face made her realize she needed to celebrate her children more often too.

RULE 70:
Let your kids help, even if it makes your life a million times harder.

Having our three-year-old help with the dishes takes three times as long as doing it alone, but she gets to learn the value of work and feel like a contributing member of the family. And we get to spend time together. When you are faced with a similar choice, remember that your children are more important than whatever the "thing" is you have to do.

RULE 71:

No matter how busy life gets, eat dinner together as a family.

This is one of those rules you have heard about for years. While it may not be news, it is so essential for a healthy family life that we could not exclude it from the book, no matter how cliché it may be. So we will leave you with just one quote from a study, and leave the application up to you.

"Studies show that the more often families eat together, the less likely kids are to smoke, drink, do drugs, get depressed, develop eating disorders, and consider suicide, and the more likely they are to do well in school, delay having sex, eat their vegetables, learn big words, and know which fork to use."[6] Sounds like this rule is worth the effort to us.

Mommy Data: Another great article on the benefits of eating dinner as a family together is by Nancy Gibbs, "The Magic of the Family Meal" (*Time Magazine*, Sunday, June 4, 2006).[7]

Helping Hands: Some great websites that encourage family dinnertime are LetsCookTonight.com and DinnerTrade.com

RULE 72:
Raise your kids to move out and move on.

You want your kids to become self-sufficient and to not move back into your basement, eat your food, and play video games all day long. There are some basic skills all functional human beings should know how to do on their own—like how to live on a budget, boil water, scramble eggs, do laundry, start a dishwasher, run a vacuum, jump a dead car battery, change a tire, make a bed, polish shoes, change a light bulb, and start a lawn mower. Don't assume that your kids will learn how to do these things by osmosis. That's why they have you. Come on, moms—don't set them loose into the world unprepared. Give them a hand while you still can. And certainly encourage them to leave home and go out on their own. I promise you they will be grateful you took the time to teach them the basic skills.

Daddy Addendum: Have your husband teach your kids the basics he is good at. You'll be surprised at everything the old man can do. (See Dad Rule 72.)

RULE 73:
Beware of what you post online.

While being active on social media (see Rule 61) is important, there is also a built-in warning. For the most part, once you post pictures and comments online and in social-media networks, it cannot be retracted, removed, or repented of. It no longer belongs to you; it is now the shared property of the World Wide Web and the millions who live in that world. So be very careful of what you post, tweet, or pin. It may come back to haunt you—and your kids.

Rule 74:

Keep learning, and share what you learn with your children.

There are so many ways to be distracted in this entertainment-at-your-fingertips age. If you are not careful, you can go years without learning anything new. Just because being Supermom is a full-time job doesn't mean you can't be engaged in learning, whether formal or informal. You can join a book club, get that degree in music performance you have always wanted, obtain that certification you have been procrastinating, or learn how to speak a different language.

But here is the key to this rule: Share what you are learning with your kids—or even better, involve them in what you are learning. For example, you can give them a copy of the book you are reading, teach them about the beauty of opera by listening to *Don Giovanni*, or teach them how to greet someone in a different language.

> *"Well, knowledge is a fine thing, and mother Eve thought so; but she smarted so severely for hers, that most of her daughters have been afraid of it since."*
>
> —Abigail Adams

RULE 75:
Make time to get lost in a good book (or movie).

Sometimes you need a little make-believe to help you escape the daily stress of motherhood and life. Find a good book and get lost within its pages, even if it's just for a few minutes here and there. You can find time to read in the most unusual places and times—like the mother who would sit outside her son's bedroom at bedtime to make sure he stayed in his room. Since she was just waiting there (sometimes for long periods of time), she would read. This, she said, started her obsession with reading. Joining a book club in your neighborhood or online will help you stay true to this rule because you will be accountable to other moms for reading.

Helping Hands: If you are interested in joining or even starting an online book club, try Goodreads.com. There are hundreds of mom book groups (clubs) to choose from.

RULE 76:
Be a facilitator of fun.

To be a facilitator of fun or coordinator of cool, you may need to dress up for Halloween, give your kids Valentines, hide Easter eggs, drive a go-cart, go caroling in the snow, or do whatever other activities your kids think are fun. Some moms have even gone paintball shooting with their offspring. While you do not have to go to this kind of extreme to be a facilitator of fun, you too can recognize what your kids consider to be fun and then supervise the experience so that it is safe, sanitary, and FUN.

RULE 77:
Never give up on your children.

Your kids will make mistakes, do dumb things, and sometimes really mess up. They're human, after all. However, if you've tried to raise them with an abundance of love, they can and will recover.

Moms, never underestimate the power of your love and the influence you have on a wayward or distressed child. Some dear friends of ours became living examples of this rule after their son was arrested on "accessory to murder" charges. Despite all their efforts to love him, teach him, and reinforce principles he had been taught growing up, he still made decisions that led him to his incarceration. They stuck with him through it all, and this rule ultimately paid off as is apparent in this excerpt from a letter he wrote: "Dad and Mom, I can hardly believe I've been in here for so long. A new man is rising, and I like him a whole lot better than the old guy. I'm so blessed to have such an awesome, loving, and support-ive family who will always be by my side. I couldn't ask more from my Heavenly Father." Remember, never give up on your children; there is always hope.

> *"And he arose, and came to his father. But when he was yet a great way off, his father saw him, and had compassion, and ran, and fell on his neck, and kissed him."*
>
> —Luke 15:20 (The parable of the prodigal son)

RULE 78:
Minimize the drama and yelling.

Regardless of the age of your children, yelling and screaming rarely accomplishes what you want it to. Yes, you may get the desired behavior in the moment, but it is only due to fear that "if we don't do as Mom says, she may start spewing fire out of her mouth." And fear only works for so long.

We remember being in the middle of a shouting match with our children where everyone was yelling and crying. Even our youngest was mimicking us by randomly yelling at his sisters. None of this was productive or desirable. Luckily, we calmed down enough to talk about how badly we had handled the situation (see Rule 33) and then agreed as a family to never yell at each other again. We discussed alternative actions we could take instead of yelling, and even role-played a couple of them. Will there be yelling and screaming in our home again? Yes, but now we at least have a common language and agreement we can come back to and use to restore order.

"Moms, even good ones, sometimes lose it a little so as not to lose it all."

—Susan Squire

RULE 79:

Remember to pamper the most important person—YOU.

Being a mother and a wife, and maybe even an employee, often means taking care of other people's needs. But if you don't take care of yourself first, you will not be able to fulfill the other roles anyway. So make time for yoga, a massage, or whatever else rejuvenates and revitalizes you. You deserve it.

Daddy Addendum: Communicate this rule clearly to your husband. He cannot read your mind, and he needs to understand what "pamper" means to you. He also needs to understand how often you need pampering and what he can do to help with this rule.

Rule 80:
Don't compare yourself to other mothers.

If you're like most moms, you may occasionally compare yourself to your mother, to your sisters, and to every other mom in the world. Don't! Comparing yourself to other mothers is not only futile but also inaccurate. Everyone has a different story, different strengths and weaknesses, and different children. As long as you are working on following some of these rules every day, you'll be just fine. Keep at it. Remember the Supermom Training Program? While it will take a lifetime to graduate, it can be a beautiful journey if you celebrate the small victories along the way.

If you are not the perfect mom yet, join the club. No mom is perfect . . . just working on a different stage. Hold your head up, sister, and remember you are powerful. You are a Superhero.

> *"The more people have studied different methods of bringing up children the more they have come to the conclusion that what good mothers and fathers feel like doing for their babies is the best after all."*
>
> —Benjamin Spock

RULE 81:

Share what you have learned with other moms.

In Rule 4, we suggested you ask other moms for help and introduced you to the power of mommy bloggers. Now it's time to return the favor. As you learn and grow as a mother, why not share these parenting nuggets with other moms? Maybe you could start your own blog or Facebook page where you share advice and real-life anecdotes. You could also mentor a new mom in the neighborhood who is too shy to apply Rule 4 herself. Maybe it's time you helped other moms recognize they have a sorority of sisters worldwide willing to help. Maybe it's time you help moms embrace their own Supermom abilities.

You can share your rules and stories with us at Rules4Families.com, and your story could be in our next edition.

RULE 82:
When you cannot find a rule to help, be creative.

Every mom is different, as are her children, and what works for one may not work for another. So when you find yourself faced with a challenging situation and you cannot find a rule to help, rely on your mother's intuition and create your own.

A mother of seven kids was tired of all the mean words, fighting, hitting, bugging, jabbing, teasing, crying, and pinching that was going on. After her attempts in traditional forms of discipline failed, she turned to her creativity and introduced her family to "The Bull"—a giant stuffed toy the size of a bean-bag chair. "From now on," she said, "there will be no more hitting and bugging each other. Starting today, you can take your aggression out by beating the bull. When you get mad, the only person you can hit is the bull." She then demonstrated by hitting the bull with a broom handle. Over the next few months the kids started to get along better. It turned out that beating up the bull was much better than beating up each other.

While this may not work for everyone, it sure helped her. What do you have in your imagination?

SOURCES

1. Changes to a woman's body after giving birth: www.babycenter.com/body-changes-after -childbirth.

2. United States Department of Agriculture: Center for Nutrition Policy and Promotion, "Miscel- laneous Publication 1528-2010," Expenditures on Children by Families. www.cnpp.usda.gov/ ExpendituresonChildrenbyFamilies.htm.

3. Student to teacher ratio: www.nces.ed.gov /programs/coe/indicator_qpt.asp

4. Pew Research Center's Internet and American Life Project, www.pewresearch.org/pubs/1484/social -media-mobile-internet-use-teens-millennials -fewer-blog, November 2011.

5. List of top adoption mommy blogs: www.circle ofMoms.com/top25/adoption

6. National Center on Addiction and Substance Abuse (CASA) at Columbia University, 2005.

7. *TIME* Magazine, Sunday, June 04, 2006 www.time.com/time/magazine/article/0,9171 ,1200760,00.html#ixzz24qzmINAI

ABOUT THE AUTHORS

Soni and Treion are the proud, sometimes cranky parents of five typical children.

Soni was raised in a traditional family in the western United States of America. Her mother is still alive and well today and is very involved in her children's lives—she's a kind woman who has always been there for her children and grandchildren, who lovingly call her "Bammie."

Soni loves the simple life. Whether enjoying the serenity of the outdoors, the exquisite tastes of different cuisine, or spending time with her family, Soni thrives on life's simple pleasures. She loves to run, eat French toast with real maple syrup and whipped cream, hike, cook for her family, take naps on the beach, and go to bed early.

Soni is also part of the singing trio Mercy River. Their self-titled debut album was released in May 2008, and their second album, *Beautiful Dawn*, was released in March of 2010. Their third album, *Higher*, was released with rave reviews in February 2012. Soni is completely in her element when she performs, and she enjoys the intimate feeling that develops as the audience connects with her music. However, despite the personal satisfaction that goes hand in hand with performing, Soni still believes that her greatest joy in life comes from being a wife and mother.

Treion, on the other hand, was raised by a single mother on the outskirts of Johannesburg, South Africa. His mother struggled her whole life to provide for her two sons, and passed away of breast cancer at the very young age of forty-three. While she never achieved any great award or made the news or accomplished any significant feat, she made a difference in the lives of her two boy's and left behind a legacy of love. To Treion and Daniel, she was a superhero.

Treion Muller is a self-proclaimed "father in motion" who moved to the United States from South Africa in 1995 to complete his bachelors and masters degrees in adult learning. He is FranklinCovey's Chief eLearning Architect, business book author, national presenter, and social media expert and online learning expert. Treion draws inspiration from his experiences as a professional dancer, medic in the South African Army, missionary, university student body president, university mascot (the Thunderbird), foster parent, and professional speaker. Treion is the author of *Dad Rules: A Simple Manual For a Complex Job* and has also coauthored two business books, *The Learning Explosion* and *The Webinar Manifesto*.

Stay in touch with Treion and Soni:

Website: Rules4Families.com
Facebook: Rules4families
Twitter: @Treeon
LinkedIn: linkedin.com/in/treionmuller

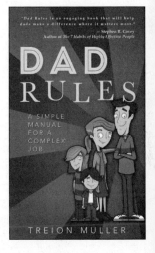